WASHINGTON, D.C.
A Scrapbook

Laura Lee Benson • illustrated by Iris Van Rynbach

ini Charlesbridge

To the memory of my grandfather, Louis Berlinsky.   L.L.B.

To the memory of my grandmother, Oma, an artist who inspired me.   I.V.R.

Table of Contents

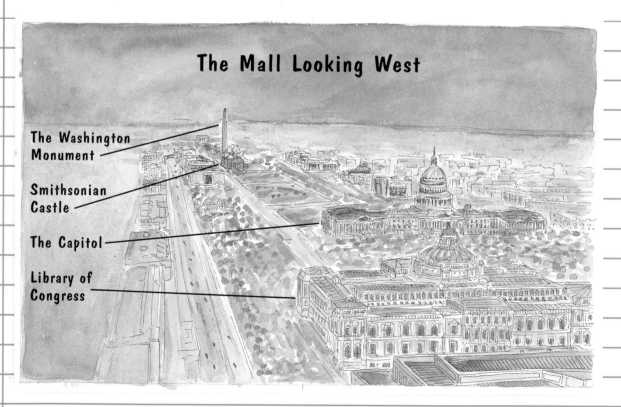

The Mall Looking West

The Washington Monument

Smithsonian Castle

The Capitol

Library of Congress

Acknowledgments:
p. 3 Amtrak®; p. 5 map and ticket courtesy of the Washington Metropolitan Area Transit Authority; pp. 7, 9 (top), 12, 13 (top), 20 all photos courtesy of www.parkphotos.com-photo #WTH027TA by Terry Adams, National Park Service, photo #TO0067 by Carol M. Highsmith, Parks & History Association, photo #MAL024PS by National Park Service, photo #SMI010CW by Chuck Wasson, Parks & History Association, photo #FO0057 by Bill Clark, National Park Service; pp. 9 (bottom), 11, 19 photos courtesy of the Library of Congress; pp. 13 (bottom), 17, 21, 22 photographs, brochure, and mementos courtesy of the Smithsonian Institution; p. 18 Claude Monet, The Artist's Garden at Vetheuil, Ailsa Mellon Bruce Collection, photograph © 1999 Board of Trustees, National Gallery of Art, Washington. The names "Amtrak" and "Smithsonian Institution" are registered trademarks and the subjects of proprietary rights used with the permission of the owners.

Hi! My name is Danny, and these are my friends Curtis, Soon-Yee, and Amanda. This is our scrapbook of a class trip we took to Washington, D.C.

We took the Amtrak® train from Philadelphia.

FUN FACT
D.C. stands for District of Columbia. It was named in honor of Christopher Columbus.

When our train arrived in the city, it pulled into a place called Union Station. It is a train station, a subway station, and a mall all in one.

Here are some things we got at the souvenir shops.

The U.S. Capitol
WASHINGTON D.C.

Washington D.C.

WASHINGTON
AMANDA
DISTRICT OF COLUMBIA

I ♥ D.C.!

Union Station was built in 1907 to accommodate inaugural crowds coming to Washington. Some people think it is one of the most beautiful train stations in the world.

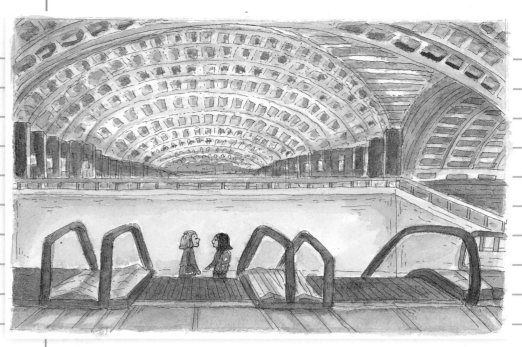

After dropping our luggage off at the hotel, we were ready to see our first sight. We boarded the Metro, the subway system that people in Washington use to get around the city.

The Metro subway system is made up of five color-coded lines that run through Washington, Maryland, and Virginia.

This is one of my Metro fare cards.

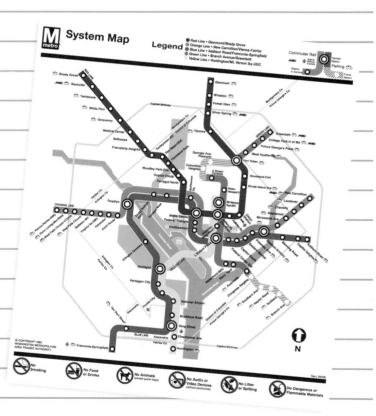

FUN FACT

The deepest Metro station has an escalator that is 230 feet high. That's about ten times higher than the average two-story house!

Our first stop was the White House. This is where the president of the United States lives. It is also where some of the most important issues in the world are discussed by the president, the president's staff, and foreign dignitaries. These talks take place in the East Room.

The White House was designed by an architect named James Hoban, who won a contest with his design. It took eight years, from 1792 to 1800, to build it. The White House has 132 rooms! That's about sixteen times as many rooms as an average house.

FUN FACT

George Washington was the only president who never got to live in the White House. His term as president was over before the White House was finished being built.

You can see a picture of the White House on the back of a twenty-dollar bill.

On our tour we saw the Green Room, the Blue Room, the Red Room, the East Room, and the State Dining Room.

FUN FACT
The State Dining Room can seat 140 dinner guests at a time!

The oldest object in the White House is a portrait of George Washington. It was saved by Dolley Madison as she and President James Madison fled the White House when it was set on fire during the War of 1812.

Behind the White House lawn is an oval-shaped park called the Ellipse. The Ellipse is a popular place for concerts and is where the national Christmas tree stands. The president lights the tree every year while crowds of people gather around to watch.

We also visited the U.S. Capitol. This is where the Senate and the House of Representatives meet to vote on bills and turn them into laws. These two branches of the government are known together as Congress.

The Senate is made up of 100 senators, two from each state. The House of Representatives is made up of 435 congressmen and congresswomen, each representing his or her own state.

If the Senate is in session during the day, a flag flies over the north end of the Capitol. If the House is in session, a flag flies over the south end of the Capitol. If they are in session at night, a light burns in the dome.

The Capitol's dome weighs nearly nine million pounds! On top of the dome is a nineteen-foot-high statue named Freedom.

On the inside of the dome is a room called the Rotunda. The curved ceiling is 180 feet high. The man who painted it had to lie on his back on a scaffold for eleven months to finish it.

THE U.S. CAPITOL

FUN FACT
The Capitol was used to house soldiers during the Civil War. The rooms were turned into living quarters and an emergency hospital.

Between the Senate and the House is an underground railroad from long ago. Today it is used as a walkway between the two wings of the Capitol.

This is the National Mall, where we stopped to eat our lunch. People use the Mall to have family picnics, fly kites, or play games like Frisbee and softball. It is also a site for festivals and political demonstrations.

One popular event held here every summer is the American Folklife Festival. It includes musicians and craftspeople from many different regions of the United States. You can also try a lot of different types of foods.

Many people also come to the Mall on the Fourth of July to watch a great fireworks display.

SMITHSONIAN CASTLE

On both sides of the Mall are many of Washington's museums. This is the Smithsonian Castle, the information center where visitors can learn about all sixteen of the Smithsonian museums.

The Mall has an antique carousel from the 1940s that still runs. Here is a picture of Curtis, Amanda, and Soon-Yee after they rode on the horses.

Smithsonian
museums

150
1846-1996
Smithsonian

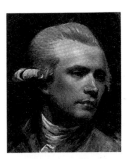

AT A-GLANCE

Washington, DC

Free brochure

Here we are at the National Museum of Natural History. It has exhibits of all kinds of animals, including dinosaurs made of real bones.

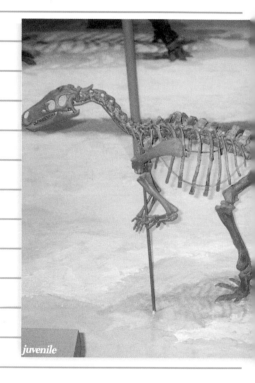

juvenile

Curtis is standing in front of a stuffed African bush elephant. It is over thirteen feet tall and weighed eight tons when it was alive. That's about the weight of eight pickup trucks!

At the Insect Zoo we saw scorpions and tarantulas being fed. I even got to hold a grasshopper that was four inches long and let it walk up my arm!

Soon-Yee's favorite thing at the museum was a seventy-million-year-old dinosaur egg. We all thought it would be pretty neat if it could still hatch.

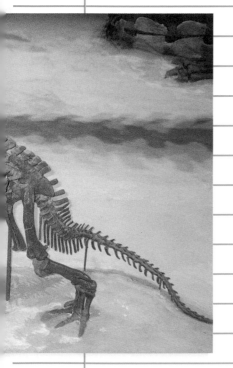

In the Discovery Room we got to touch bones, shells, and fossils.

Next we went to my favorite museum, the National Air and Space Museum. It is visited by over ten million people each year. It is filled with space shuttles, satellites, old airplanes, and moon rocks.

You can see one of the first all-metal planes, the Northrop Alpha with TWA markings. Built in the 1930s, it could carry up to four passengers in a heated cabin, but the pilot had to sit behind them in a cold, open cockpit.

FUN FACT
You can climb into some of the exhibits! We got to walk through a backup Skylab space station and see the astronauts' living quarters.

Here is a picture of me standing next to an astronaut's space suit.

We also got to look through a model of the Hubble Space Telescope and see a duplicate of the Apollo 11 command module.

FREEZE-DRIED ICE CREAM

CHOCOLATE • VANILLA • STRAWBERRY
SPACE FOOD

READY TO EAT
PLEASE DO NOT
OPEN INSIDE MUSEUM

NATIONAL AIR & SPACE MUSEUM
WASHINGTON, D.C.

NET WT. 3/4

There is a special theater called IMAX that is five stories high. When you watch the movies you feel like you're in them!

We saw a planetarium show where we learned about constellations.

EINSTEIN PLANETARIUM
The Stars Tonight

8:00 PM   YOUTH
ADMISSION

National Air and Space Museum
Smithsonian Institution

Here is a wrapper from a package of freeze-dried astronaut food that I bought in the gift shop. YUM!

Washington has many art museums. This is the National Gallery of Art. It has one of the most important collections of artwork in the world. Some pictures are so valuable that you can only see them by making an appointment first.

The National Gallery of Art has two buildings: the West Building and the East Building. The West Building contains older artwork by world-famous artists like Leonardo da Vinci and Claude Monet. The East Building contains modern art by artists like M.C. Escher and Alexander Calder.

FUN FACT

In between the two buildings is a moving walkway in an underground tunnel. As you move along the walkway, you can see a glassed-in waterfall that is actually the underside of an outdoor fountain.

On the next part of our trip, we visited some famous landmarks. This is the Washington Monument, the highest monument in the city. It is 555 feet high.

At the base of the Washington Monument are fifty American flags, one for each state.

It is the highest masonry structure in the world.

Inside there is a winding staircase with 897 steps. For safety reasons, visitors must use the elevator to get to the top. We rode to the top and could see the whole city down below!

FUN FACT

The base of the monument is a slightly different color than the rest of it. That is because the builders ran out of money during the construction. When they had enough money to finish it, the stone available was a different shade.

Here is a picture of the Washington Monument under construction.

The next monument we saw was the Lincoln Memorial, built to remember our nation's sixteenth president, Abraham Lincoln.

Inscriptions of Lincoln's Gettysburg Address can be seen on the walls on each side of the statue.

FUN FACT

Lincoln's statue is nineteen feet high, more than three times as tall as an average man.

In 1963 Martin Luther King Jr. gave his famous "I Have a Dream" speech on the steps of the Lincoln Memorial.

The Vietnam Veterans' Memorial is another important monument in Washington.

NATIONAL ZOOLOGICAL PARK

Our last stop was the National Zoological Park. It is home to more than five thousand animals. Many of the animals are endangered species.

EXPLORE AMAZONIA AT THE NATIONAL ZOO.

FONZ · FRIENDS OF THE NATIONAL ZOO

Amazonia is a re-creation of a tropical rain forest that you can walk through.

In the Reptile Discovery Center you can investigate reptiles and amphibians up close.

At the Think Tank, visitors can communicate with orangutans and gorillas through a computer.

The O Line is a cable system in the park that lets orangutans travel freely between buildings. You can see orangutans right above your head!

One of the zoo's most popular animals is Hsing-Hsing, the panda. He was given as a gift to America's children by the People's Republic of China in 1972.

Making a Scrapbook

My class trip to Washington was a great adventure. I hope you had fun learning about it. Maybe you can make a scrapbook for the next special trip you take. Here's how:

1. Buy a small notebook or tablet.
2. Collect special mementos and postcards from your visits.
3. Take lots of pictures.
4. Tape or glue the mementos, postcards, and pictures into your notebook in the order of your trip.
5. Make special notes to remember things you saw and did.
6. Share your new scrapbook with a friend!

Taking Pictures

Here are some tips for taking the best possible pictures:

1. Stand with the sun behind you so that it is shining on the subject you are photographing.
2. Make sure your subject is centered when you look through the lens.
3. Hold the camera firmly when you click the shutter.

You can take good photos like this one of the Capitol if you follow my tips!

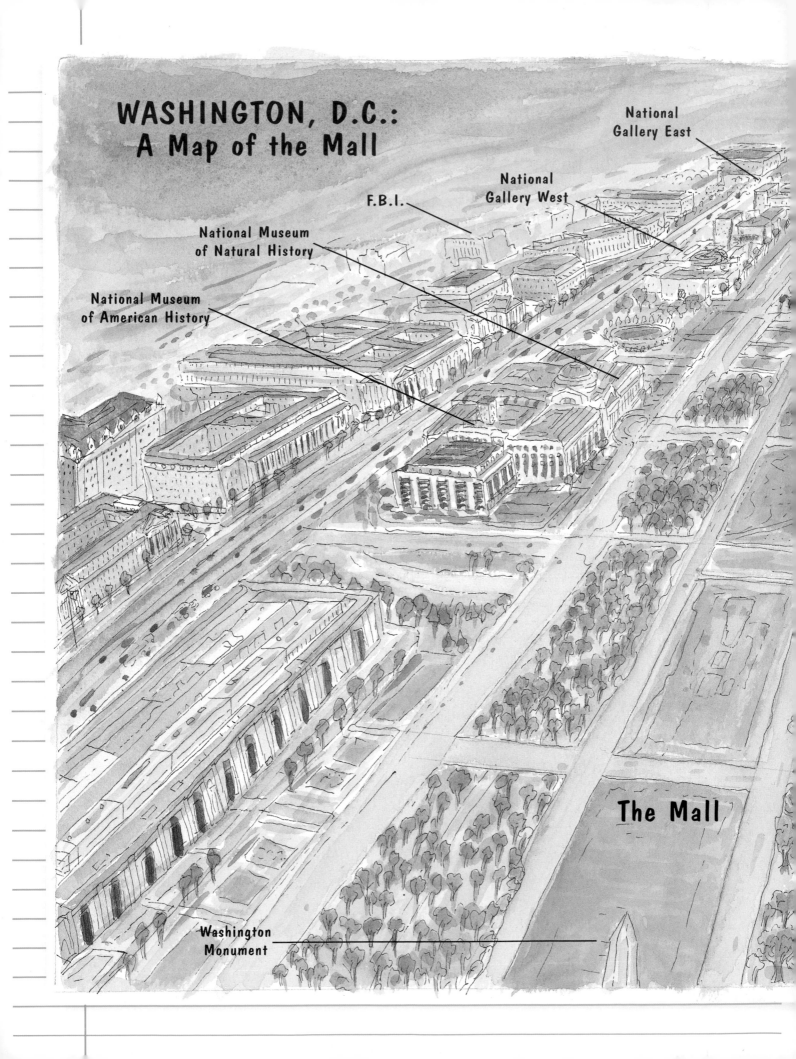

WASHINGTON, D.C.:
A Map of the Mall

National Gallery East

National Gallery West

F.B.I.

National Museum of Natural History

National Museum of American History

The Mall

Washington Monument

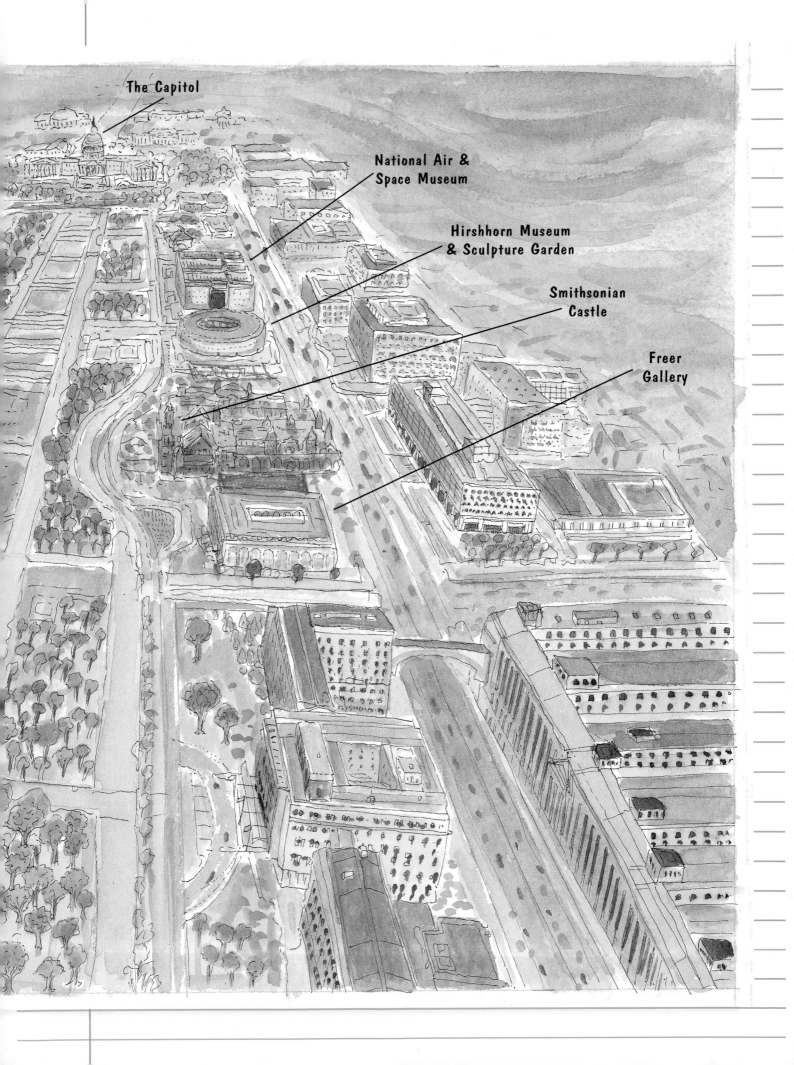

The Capitol

National Air &
Space Museum

Hirshhorn Museum
& Sculpture Garden

Smithsonian
Castle

Freer
Gallery

The History of Washington, D.C.

Washington, D.C., was many things before it became the nation's capital. In the 1600s the Washington area was inhabited by Native Americans. The Nanticoke, Piscataway, and Powhatan tribes raised vegetables, fished, and made tools and pottery. In the late 1600s and early 1700s European settlers came to America. They grew tobacco and started a trading port. In the 1800s Washington, D.C., became the home of the nation's government. In 1812 the U.S. went to war with Great Britain, and in 1814 British forces stormed the city and burned the Capitol, the White House, and other public buildings, so they had to be rebuilt. Today Washington is a thriving city, with many of its original buildings still intact.

The Supreme Court Building

How the United States Government Works

The government consists of three separate branches:

1. The legislative branch, which is Congress, makes the laws.
2. The judicial branch, which is the Supreme Court, interprets the laws.
3. The executive branch, which is led by the president, carries out the laws.

Congress is composed of the Senate and the House of Representatives, which hold their meetings in separate wings of the Capitol building. The primary duties of Congress are to examine and pass laws.

The Supreme Court is made up of nine judges who work to uphold the Constitution, the laws by which all Americans abide. The judges are asked to decide whether rulings made in other courts are correct.

The president's cabinet is made up of fourteen people who run the executive branch of the federal government. These cabinet members advise the president on different areas of government. The vice president is also part of the executive branch. If the president is unable to continue working, the vice president takes over the office.

Washington, D.C.: A Time Line

1750

1783: The United States Congress, located in Philadelphia, Pennsylvania, decided to establish a federal city for the United States government.

1791: George Washington, the nation's first president, picked the site taking land from Maryland and Virginia.

1792: Construction of the White House and Capitol began.

1800: The nation's government moved from Philadelphia to Washington, D.C. John Adams became the first president to live in the White House.

1812–1815: The War of 1812 took place. Many government buildings were burned down by British troops.

1850

1862: Congress outlawed slavery in Washington.

1865: Four years after the Civil War began, President Abraham Lincoln was assassinated by John Wilkes Booth at Ford's Theatre.

1866: Congress granted African-American men in Washington the right to vote.

1881: President James Garfield was assassinated at a Washington, D.C. railroad station.

1900

1917: The United States entered World War I. Many people came to Washington to support the war effort.

1932: As the Great Depression reached its peak, more than twenty thousand World War I veterans, some with their families, camped in Washington to protest their desperate condition.

1933: President Franklin D. Roosevelt created the New Deal to help the United States get out of the Depression. More jobs were created through this program, so Washington's population grew again.

1950

1963: Dr. Martin Luther King Jr. led 200,000 people to the steps of the Lincoln Memorial for the March on Washington civil rights demonstration.

1969: In a protest against the Vietnam War, 250,000 people marched in Washington.

1995: The Million Man March, a gathering of about 1.5 million African-American men, took place on the Mall as an expression of atonement and reconciliation among African-American communities.

2000

Museums to See

1. Ford's Theatre and Lincoln Museum
   511 Tenth Street, NW
   Stop by this historic landmark to learn about the night of President Lincoln's assassination and visit the museum, which houses artifacts that belonged to the president.

2. The Capital Children's Museum
   800 Third Street, NE
   Experience exhibits you can touch, smell, hear, and taste!

3. The Hirshhorn Museum and Sculpture Garden
   Independence Avenue and Seventh Street, SW
   See this unique collection of modern art, including a wall mosaic made of pieces of old toys.

4. The National Air and Space Museum
   Independence Avenue and Seventh Street, SW
   See the most visited museum in the world, filled with an incredible collection of space and travel artifacts.

5. The National Museum of American Art
   Eighth and G Streets, NW
   Visit this museum to see some interesting folk art, including a fiberglass cowboy and a giraffe made of soda-bottle caps.

6. The National Museum of African Art
   950 Independence Avenue, SW
   Experience the Folktales from Africa storytelling session, or the Workshops for Families, where you can make African crafts.

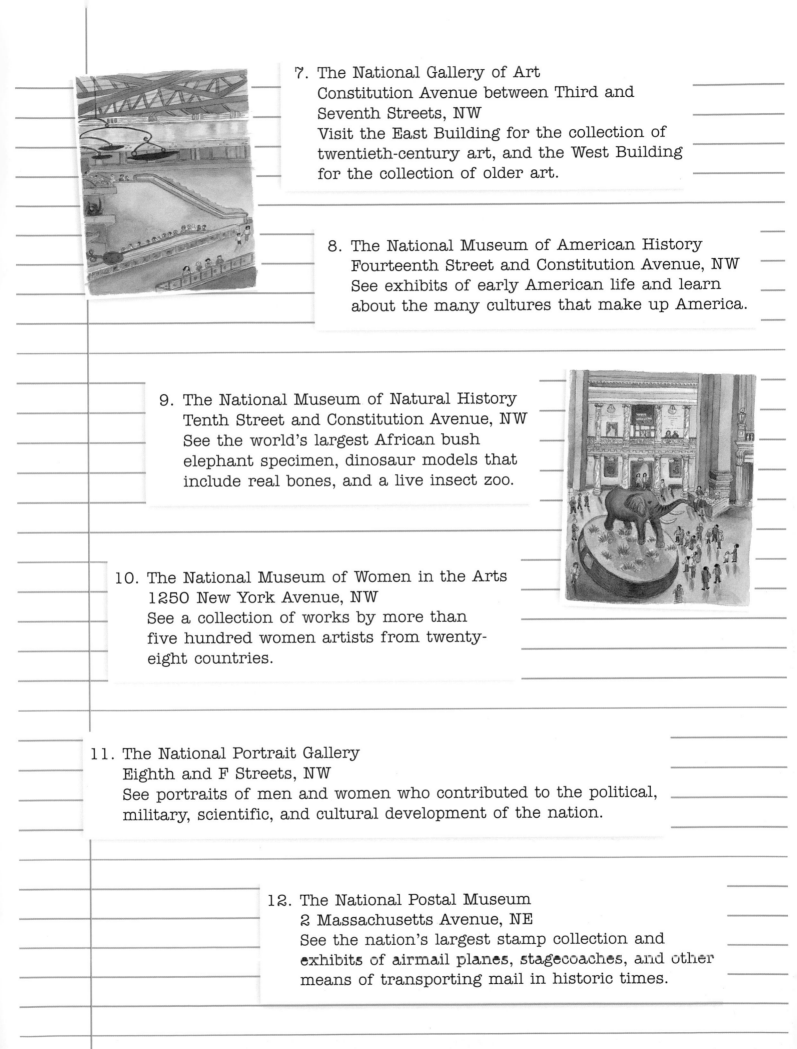

7. The National Gallery of Art
   Constitution Avenue between Third and
   Seventh Streets, NW
   Visit the East Building for the collection of
   twentieth-century art, and the West Building
   for the collection of older art.

8. The National Museum of American History
   Fourteenth Street and Constitution Avenue, NW
   See exhibits of early American life and learn
   about the many cultures that make up America.

9. The National Museum of Natural History
   Tenth Street and Constitution Avenue, NW
   See the world's largest African bush
   elephant specimen, dinosaur models that
   include real bones, and a live insect zoo.

10. The National Museum of Women in the Arts
    1250 New York Avenue, NW
    See a collection of works by more than
    five hundred women artists from twenty-
    eight countries.

11. The National Portrait Gallery
    Eighth and F Streets, NW
    See portraits of men and women who contributed to the political,
    military, scientific, and cultural development of the nation.

12. The National Postal Museum
    2 Massachusetts Avenue, NE
    See the nation's largest stamp collection and
    exhibits of airmail planes, stagecoaches, and other
    means of transporting mail in historic times.

Cultural Sites to See

1. Frederick Douglass's National Historic Site
   1411 W Street, SE
   Visit this former residence of Frederick Douglass, an African-American abolitionist.

2. The United States Holocaust Memorial Museum
   100 Raoul Wallenberg Place, SW
   This museum memorializes the six million Jews and the millions of others who were killed during the Holocaust.

3. The Thomas Jefferson Memorial
   Fifteenth Street on the Tidal Basin, SW
   See this grand statue of Thomas Jefferson and read the Declaration of Independence on the walls around him.

4. The John F. Kennedy Center for the Performing Arts
   2700 F Street, NW
   See flags from every state and every nation in the world, and see unique gifts that have been given to the United States from foreign nations.

5. The Korean War Veterans Memorial
   Daniel French Drive and Independence Avenue, NW
   This memorial, designed to honor the soldiers killed during the Korean War, displays nineteen figures representing some of the different ethnic backgrounds of the soldiers involved in this war.

6. The Library of Congress
   First and Independence Avenue, SE
   Visit the world's largest library, which contains books, photos, prints, maps, video and audio recordings, and famous writings.

7. The Lincoln Memorial
   Twenty-third Street at Constitution and Independence Avenue, NW
   See this impressive memorial to Abraham Lincoln and read the famous Gettysburg Address on the walls around him.

8. The Vietnam Veterans Memorial
   Constitution Avenue at Henry Bacon Drive, NW
   Visit this memorial and see the names of more than
   58,000 men and women who died during the Vietnam War.

9. The Washington National Cathedral
   Massachusetts Avenue at Wisconsin Avenue
   This sixth-largest Gothic cathedral in the
   world offers a panoramic view of Washington
   from the observatory in its west tower.

10. The White House
    1600 Pennsylvania Avenue, NW
    See where the president of the
    United States lives and works, and
    tour the rooms open to visitors.

11. Union Station
    50 Massachusetts Avenue, NE
    This transportation center and shopping mall is surrounded by beautiful
    architecture, including barrel-vaulted ceilings, statues, and columns.

12. U.S. Capitol
    East End of the National Mall
    Visit this important building to see
    where the House and Senate vote
    on bills and turn bills into laws.

13. U.S. Supreme Court
    First and Capitol Streets, NE
    Visit the highest court in the country, where cases
    are decided by the nine judges of the Court, who
    work to uphold the United States Constitution.

Resources for Planning a Trip to Washington, D.C.

Places to Write or Call

D.C. Chamber of Commerce
Suite 309
1301 Pennsylvania Avenue, NW
Washington, D.C. 20004
(202) 638-3222

Washington Visitor Information Center

1455 Pennsylvania Avenue, NW
Washington, D.C. 20004
(202) 789-7038

Books for Further Reading

Clark, Diane C. *A Kid's Guide to Washington, D.C.* Gulliver Books, 1996.

Fradin, Dennis. *Washington, D.C.* Children's Press, 1992.

Frommer's Washington, D.C., with Kids. Macmillan, 1998.

Levy, Debbie. *Kidding around Washington, D.C.:
A Fun Filled, Fact Packed Travel and Activity Book.* John Muir Publications, 1997.

Reef, Catherine. *Washington, D.C.* Macmillan, 1990.

Steins, Richard. *Our National Capital.* I Know America. Millbrook Press, 1994.

WWW Sites for Kids:

http://www.ipl.org/youth/stateknow/dc1.html
http://www.moneyfactory.com
http://www.si.edu.organiza/museum/zoo/start.htm
http://www.amnh.org/explore/index.html
http://www.nasm.si.edu

WWW Sites for Parents:

http://city.net/countries/united_states_/district_of_columbia
http://www.washington.org
http://dcpages.ari.net
http://www.si.edu

Library of Congress Cataloging-in-Publication Data
Benson, Laura Lee, 1963—
Washington D.C.: a scrapbook/Laura Lee Benson;
illustrated by Iris Van Rynbach.
    p.   cm.
Summary: Describes a class tour of Washington, D.C.,
and provides information about museums,
monuments, government buildings, and cultural sites
in a scrapbook format. Includes a historical time line.
    ISBN 0-88106-064-X (reinforced for library use)
    ISBN 0-88106-063-1 (softcover)
1. Washington (D.C.)—Description and travel—
Juvenile literature. 2. Washington (D.C.)—Tours—
Juvenile literature. [1. Washington (D.C.)—
Description and travel.] I. Van Rynbach, Iris, ill.
II. Title. III. Title: Washington, D.C.
F194.3.B46   1999
917.5304'41—dc21   98-53799
[E]

Printed in South Korea
(hc) 10 9 8 7 6 5 4 3 2 1
(sc) 10 9 8 7 6 5 4 3 2 1

Published by Charlesbridge Publishing
85 Main Street, Watertown, MA 02472
(617) 926-0329
www.charlesbridge.com

The illustrations in this book were done in
watercolor on Arches watercolor paper.
The display type and text type were set in
American Typewriter and Dom Casual.
Color separations were made by Eastern Rainbow,
Derry, New Hampshire.
Printed and bound by Sung In Printing, Inc.,
South Korea
Production supervision by Brian G. Walker
Designed by Diane M. Earley